Girl over the moon ,
on sands of time

Kshipra Moreker

BookLeaf Publishing

India | USA | UK

Presentation by *BookLeaf Publishing*

Web: www.bookleafpub.com

E-mail: info@bookleafpub.com

ISBN: 9789363303317

First edition 2024

To my mother Mrs Rohini Pethe, and my father who never gave up on me, his sister Dr Shilpa Moreker and her husband Mr Amit Vyas, his cousin Mrs Harsha Mehta and her husband Mr Hemendra Mehta, my father's brother Dr Mayur Moreker, their biology school teacher Mrs Devika Shetty and her husband Mr Sadanand Shetty and their daughter Dr Deepa Shetty and my friends Niyati Panicker, Parisa Kaur, Svara Dave, Niara Mishra, Raisa and her mother and grandparents who are always there for me and Nandini Rajawade as well as Keya Hatkar who are my inspiration

ACKNOWLEDGEMENT

Dr Mrs Swati Popat
Dr Mrs Vandana Lulla
Dr Mrs Rekha Bajaj
Dr Manoj Agny and family
Dr Usha Johari and family
Advocate Mrs Usha Purohit
Ms Divya Dutta and family
Mr Sairam Iyer
Mr Savio Soares
Mr Sarvesh Bhardwaj
Ms Rekha Balgi and Girish ji
Mrs Mangala Rajawade and family
Dr Harish Hosalkar and family
Dr Amaresh Jadumani
Dr Nilesh Panchal and family
Dr Ashutosh Nerurkar and family
Dr Ravindran Tannameni and Sankara hospital Vishakhapatnam
Rohini Vadera sister and Raheja hospital nurses
Dr Shilpa Patil and Apollo hospital Belapur family
Dr Harshvardhan Ghorpade and family
Dr Mahesh Uparkar and family
Dr Jyoti and all doctors at Fortis Hiranandani hospital

PREFACE

She gazed on to the moon and saw many things. As a young child, it was a rabbit on the moon, as she heard lullabies of the moon becaming a mama (uncle). As she grew older, she knew that India had landed on the moon and she learnt about the craters, the far side and the minerals on the moon, and also how moon tubes could be used as a Noah's arc to store the genetic material which would be lost from the genetic bank at Svalbard as the waters would rise and flood it all.

And then she looked beyond the moon. She looked at the moons of Jupiter and Saturn and then at moons of earth like exoplanets, millions of light years away in some habitable zones of some other start of some other galaxy in some other constellation..

Moon at One

"Mumma, Babba" is all she could say
Then the wind made the leaves sway
And a ball peeked in, only to hide away
And all her father would say..

Moon, moon, don't go away,
Little baby wants to play
Leaves, leaves, of the trees in the way,
Let the breeze make you sway

Little baby won't eat, till you say
Don't worry, baby, I am here to stay
Hide and seek is what we will play
That is how you will make my day

The moon at times goes away
Only to rise again someday
Letting the little baby say
If it's gone, it's not gone forever away

That is how the baby learnt to say
Never will anything truly go away

No Moon Blues

The night was dark, and all that was heard was a
dog's bark
Gloom hung in the sky, there was no moon, was
that why?

No moon-day was just one way to say
That the girl could not see any way
Life stood still without a hopeful ray
Would cancer take her mother? doctors couldn't
say

The heart bled tears of pain
All prayers seemed to go in vain
Nothing made sense to the brain
Tears through the night left the pillow stained

Will she live, will she not ..
Can someone invent a bot
To tell the child, "Fear not
Your mother will soon be next to you in your
cot"

"The moon will be back soon, dear"
So said the father, calming her fear
As the crescent began to appear
So was slowly back home, Mumma dear

Moon in Shadow

Moon was what all had praised
The moon brought love in the words they said
With the moon eclipsed, everything went dark
It was turn for the dogs to bark

She heard about the moon in shadow
She went out looking for it in the meadow
And all she saw was a creeping commando
And suddenly, everything was in shadow

The guns went off and the roses fell
Who is friend and who is foe, you couldn't tell
Bodies strewn all over the place
Humanity was lost in any case

Hatred raised its ugly face
As towards hell they all race
Little hands clutched their mothers' dress
The mothers holding babies to their breast

Soon, all lay lifeless
Not a single soul to bless
Eerie night had only one thing to stress
Let the moon be back with a smiling face

Twice in a blue moon

Twice in a blue moon, the Earth shatters
And I find a night when I'm in tatters
It's more often than just once
I know in my heart I'll always bounce

Twice in a blue moon, I didn't bounce
I had in me courage, not even one ounce
The dark clouds waiting upon me to pounce
And I waited for that fatal blow to trounce

And then there were those amazing clowns
That appeared from nowhere to wipe off my
frowns
Wearing those colourful happy gowns
Bringing me up from my life's lowest downs

Twice in a blue moon, for every down, there
were many clowns
Twice in a blue moon, I lost my frowns
Twice in a blue moon, the blues were gone
Twice in a blue moon, I decided for someone
else....that clown

Harvest Moon

Harvest moon, Harvest moon
The harvest is yet to bloom
Have you arrived too soon?
Harvest moon, Harvest moon

Harvest moon, Harvest moon
You are such a wonderful boon
But for those over the desert dune
You don't exist, my dear moon

Harvest moon, Harvest moon
There is someone they call a loon
When you increase the ocean tide
The loon's antics no longer hide

Harvest moon, Harvest moon
Be it loon or one over the dune
Everyone waits for you to come soon
Harvest moon, Harvest moon

The Tween's moon

Tweens are before we become the teens
Not many know what it means
But a tween is what I have been
And so I know that's when we are Queens

Teens have their special moon
You won't find it in the TV toons
Take your binocs and gaze up high
Special is the tween moon and you will know
why

The tween looks up with starry eyes
Gazing far into the sky
Falling stars are passing by
Telling stories of the galaxies gone by

The Tween doesn't feel so shy
When the tweens gazes into the sky
Never will the tween ever cry
If the tween moon is shining bright in the sky

Full moon, Half Moon, Full Moon

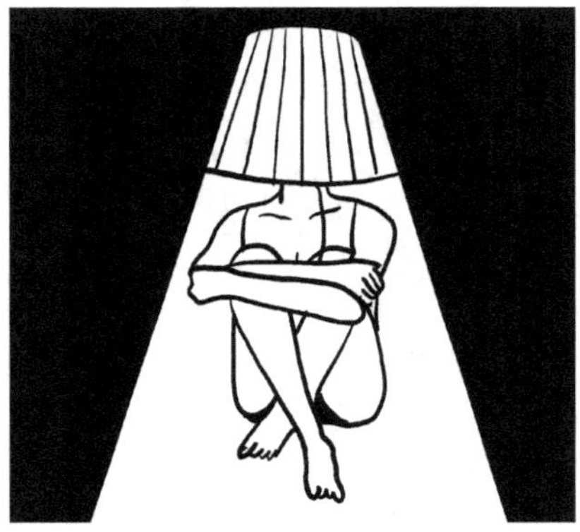

Full moon became half moon
I am down in the dune
Wondering if I will be gone soon
In my sky there will be no moon

They always thought I was a cartoon
To make them laugh I acted like a loon
Now it has been a while
Since my face adorned a smile

Lived not for self but for others
But no one bothers
Their ignorance feels like a million smothers
Such is the life of those abandoned by own
mothers

As the zeal for life did wane
How could one remain sane
Everything seemed in vain
End it all....says the Brain

The sun comes around shining light
I ain't going to give up without a fight
That one thing what one sees in the night
Of the waxing moon in plain sight

No moon will become half moon
Half moon will become Full Moon
Every soul that's given up will understand soon
That waxing back in form is your boon

No moon, half moon, Full Moon
Full moon, half moon, No moon
And again, No moon, half moon, Full moon
Moon or no moon, let your face be the moon

Be the Moon that will light up the life
Of those who have lost everything in strife
Full moon, full moon
Be their boon, be their boon

Journey to the moon

We are going to the moon
To the moon, to the moon
Landing there real soon
We are going to the moon

Neil, Edwin, and Buzz
All serious and no fuss
Fires of doubt they will douse
Inspired will be every house

Soon the world will follow
Three men aboard Apollo
Fear is what they will swallow
As they land on the moon with Apollo

As they bid their families a long goodbye
And set off on their mission to fly
Not once wondering whether they would die
As they soared far, far up into the sky

They went, and took human pride along
In their hearts, was that sprightly song
Here we come.. ting tong... tong tong
Taking long strides like King Kong

Teen moon

The moon for the teen
What does it mean
As soon as its seen
The teen will be at the scene

With love brimming to the seam
You know, all of us have there been
It's all there in every human's genes
Causing raging, flowing..oxytocin

And while dealing with the zits
And the times when one is in the pits
And confidence coming in pieces and bits
One learns never to call it quits

Holding hands with the one
Glowing as if one is none other than the Sun
The teen is seen under the moon
With someone over whom the teen is ready to
swoon

Looking at the moon to learn
Finding someone worthy to yearn
Living dreams right out of stories of Jules Verne
Relationships are what the teen learns to earn

Blood moon

Blood moon is what I have been
That's when I am never seen
The face blushes deep red
As I am hiding in my bed

The bloom in me is quite eclipsed
Yet there shines a part of me, at the edge
Proudly wearing that shiny badge
That the teacher trusted I would manage

The moon becomes a beaver..
And I become a story weaver ..
And one becomes what one choses
To get it done or hide in excuses

And as the blood moon comes out of it
I find the courage to do my bit
And everything begins to fit
To a life of hard work is what I commit

India at the moon

Americans were first at the moon
The rest of the world was there soon
It was the beginning of the race
To bring a smile on the ruler's face

The Soviet flag flew on the moon
China too joined them soon
And just when it was to be Japan
India too, landed at the moon

But not before we overcame our fear
And shed for failure a millionth tear
Finding the moon so far yet so near
And as one crashed, we sighed, "Oh dear"

India too reached the moon
And will explore the other side soon
Making it for humanity, a boon
Minerals, water and more, it will find soon

Gene Bank On the Moon

Noah had every species bailed
And through the flood, we safely sailed
Today we have it underground
Every living thing will be found

Underground at Svalbard is where it's all
But climate change will flood it all
The ice will melt and swell the seas
The air won't have the oxygen from the trees

Moon tubes are the place where it can be
As safe as ever, keep it, could we
It ain't as simple as it might seem
To keep quite safe, every species' gene

Moon in the rain

Moon in the rain is every bard's gain
Whether the bard is happy or in pain
Peeking from between the clouds
It waters every soul's mental drought

Holding hands, watching the moon & the rains
Heartbeats racing in a steady gain
The breeze lightly caressing the skin
And the divine feeling slowly sinks in

Moonlight sojourns in night
With rains ...oh.. what a sight!
When things eventually turn out right
And you forget why did you ever fight

Moon in the rain, moon in the rain
Soothing my heart and my brain
Makes the hearts come closer
Relationships grow stronger

Moon gazing

Time takes everything in its stride
Lost are the waves you always ride
No one waits for anyone, not time, not tide
But the moon always remains by my side

It looks at me in various ways
Makes me always, at it, gaze
Takes me into a slight daze
Watching it watch me, days on days

I wonder what it wants to say
In a subtle and silent way
As I wach it from the bay
It has words in every single ray

Many more it has spoken to before me
Peeping in and out of the tree
Leaving no conditions, just let it be
In different ways will each one see

The moon will change with every gaze
The world will cease to be a maze
When one is lost in a mortal daze
Then come to me is what the moon says..

Moon, the eternal witness to my undying friendships

Life is a stage they say....we're here for a show...
The stars in the sky an audience, the moon
bearing witness to everything high and low...

The actors leave one by one, making us wonder
if it's time to go...
Without loved ones around, life feels really low

On by one, all of them, do they go ...
Some by death, some who let you forego ...
It's only friends who remain ....no matter what
in life will come and go
Friends like the moon, who get back within you
... that glow .....

So when it's possible, don't let that chance go
Gratitude and respect is all you can show...
Let your friend know....let your friend know...
What is it to them that you owe .....

Moon is drifting away

The moon is drifting away, drifting away
That is what the scientists seem to say
An hour more gets added to the day
More time at hand, but people far away

Distance makes the heart grow fonder
Is it always like that? I ponder
Far and wide as I wander
In the tears of my loved ones, I flounder

Will I see some of them ever, I wonder
Amidst economic lightening and thunder
Emotions are something one cannot launder
Hiding oneself as on prowl is the Sounder

As each keeps their head above water
The world becomes much hotter
And not just the moon that wanders
Relationships begin to flounder

Moon gaze

Observe the moon, long enough in the gaze
Be it a bright clear night or one in a haze
Be it with a clear mind or one with emotions
ablaze
Let watching the moon become your craze

Sometimes I watch it intensely, at times in a
daze
Sometimes it's low, sometimes your eyes have
to raise
Sometimes, like your mind, it appears in a glaze
Sometimes it is smooth, sometimes it's goes
through a fraze

All of it may be real or just in your mind
Ask a peer, and the reality you shall find
In raptures will it capture you and bind
In the end, it will render you soft and kind

That is what it will do to your mind
Yourself is what you will find
And you know you have always been blind
The world in the moon will you find

Moon craters

Mysterious markings on the moon
Some call it a hare prancing around
Some call it a Goddess bathing in a pool
Crater is what the astronomer will say

Does it hurt itself when it hides in the day
The scientists vehemently say, "Nay, nay!"
It hurts itself in the night and day
When the asteroids and meteors, its surface they
fray

A luminous disc, a celestial pearl
A shining sentinel like an earl
A lantern in the sky illuminating the world
You did take the hits to protect the world

The craters are a reason for us to be grateful
Our days would be numbered and nights tearful
Had you let those rocks pass through
And let them make the Earth brew

Craters, craters, is not what I will say
Look down upon them, no way
Whenever I look up at you in the sky
Remember will I, death passed us by

Moon and me tomorrow

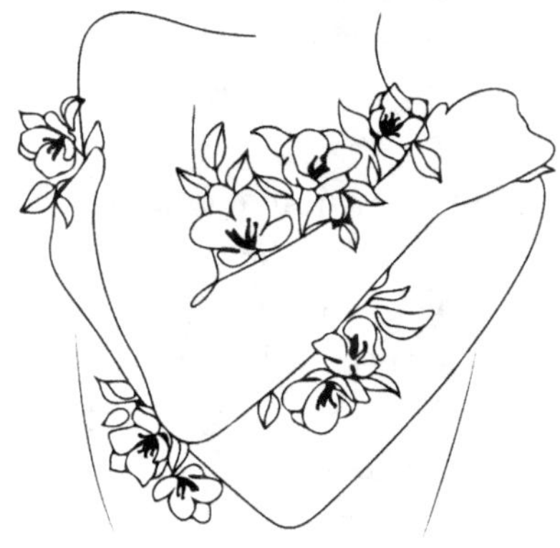

Did the moon play with your daughter?
This is what I asked her
And she replied, "Aren't you my past?"
I started wondering how she got here so fast

Yes, there she was with her kid
I just know not what she did
To travel back in time
This future self of mine

She remembers the lullaby my mom sung
Was she truly in her past hung
Those rhymes to far had I flung
Nowhere near to find those words on my tongue

Yes, but when she had a child
She went literally wild
Singing away her heart those rhymes
Rembering the long-lost times

Yes, it was me I saw from the future
Staring at me now, right here
Her face bold and without fear
As she wiped away a falling tear

Her parents were gone
She was deeply worn
After her kid was born
Her heart felt literally torn

She longed for everyone
But couldn't find anyone
What remained was the moon
Her extremely treasured boon

Eternal moon

It was there when I was a child with her granny
It was there when came my nanny
It was there when I became a nanny
It was there when I became a granny

It shone as bright as ever
Leave my side? It would never
Having it around made me braver
Knowing more about it made me clever

It has been around for centuries
It has seen innumerable stories
Hiding in between the trees
Being always on life's playscreen

Millions will come and go
To The lost, it will paths show
To The lovers, it will glow
It will shower its light as the rivers flow

Ode to the moon

Moon, oh moon, do tell the future my story
Shine as you always do, in all your glory
Human lives and their potpourri
And a billion lives portrayed in your story

The disc in the sky will always remind me why
I have to bow to the sentinel high in the sky
To many Earths and its heavens I may fly
But to you, dear moon, I will never say goodbye

Never say bye, never say bye
The ode to the moon will never be a lie
It will for eternity shine
And to everyone it will say, "Don't worry, you
will be fine"
Don't worry, you will be fine